MW00987540

bridges to contemplative living
with thomas merton

one:
entering the school of your experience

edited by jonathan montaldo & robert g. toth
of the merton institute for contemplative living

ave maria press AmP notre dame, indiana

Ave Maria Press acknowledges the permission of the following publishers for use of excerpts from the following books:

Conjectures of a Guilty Bystander by Thomas Merton, copyright © 1966 by the Abbey of Gethsemani. Used by permission of Doubleday, a division of Random House, Inc.

Contemplative Prayer by Thomas Merton, originally published as *The Climate of Monastic Prayer,* copyright © 1969 by Cistercian Publications. Used by permission of Cistercian Publications.

The Hidden Ground of Love by Thomas Merton, copyright © 1985 by The Merton Legacy Trust. Used by permission of Farrar, Straus & Giroux.

The Jerusalem Community Rule of Life by Pierre-Marie Delfieux. Translated from the French by Kathleen England. Copyright ©1985, Paulist Press, Inc., New York, Mahwah, NJ. Used with permission. www.paulistpress.com

New Seeds of Contemplation, copyright © 1961 by The Abbey of Gethsemani. Reprinted by permission of New Directions Publishing Corp.

The Psalms, A New Translation, arranged by Joseph Gelineau, copyright © 1966 by Paulist Press, Inc. , New York, Mahwah, NJ. Used with permission. www.paulistpress.com

The Spiral Staircase: My Climb Out of Darkness by Karen Armstrong, copyright © 2004 by Karen Armstrong. Used by permission of Alfred A. Knopf, a division of Random House, Inc.

Founded in 1865, Ave Maria Press is a ministry of the Indiana Province of Holy Cross.

www.avemariapress.com

ISBN-10 1-59471-089-9   ISBN-13 978-1-59471-089-6

Cover and text design by Andy Wagoner

Cover photograph © Robert Hill Photography

Interior photograph; Zen Garden, Gethsemani, 1967, by Thomas Merton. Used with permission of the Merton Legacy Trust and the Thomas Merton Center at Bellarmine University. Interior photograph of Thomas Merton on p.7 by John Lyons. Used with permission of the Merton Legacy Trust.

Printed and bound in the United States of America.

E ither you look at the universe as a
very poor creation out of which
no one can make anything, or you look
at your own life and your own part in
the universe as infinitely rich, full of
inexhaustible interest, opening out
into the infinite further possibilities for
study and contemplation and praise.
Beyond all and in all is God.

THOMAS MERTON
JULY 17, 1956

A NOTE ABOUT INCLUSIVE LANGUAGE

Thomas Merton wrote at a time before inclusive language was common practice. In light of his inclusive position on so many issues and his references to our essential unity, we hope these texts will be read from an inclusive point of view.

CONTENTS

INTRODUCTION

WHAT DO WE MEAN BY CONTEMPLATIVE LIVING?

Life is a spiritual journey. Contemplative living is a way of responding to our everyday experiences by consciously attending to our relationships. It deepens the awareness of our connectedness and communion with others, becomes a positive force of change in our lives, and provides meaningful direction to our journey. Ultimately, contemplative living leads us to a sense of well-being, profound gratitude, and a clearer understanding of our purpose in life.

Living contemplatively begins with ourselves but leads us in the end to embrace deeply not only our truest self, but God, neighbor, and all of creation. By reflecting on our everyday experiences, we seek the depths of our inner truth. By exploring our beliefs, illusions, attitudes and assumptions, we find our true self and discover how we relate to the larger community. Contemplative living directs our minds and hearts to the truly important issues of human existence, making us less likely to be captivated by the superficial distractions that so easily occupy our time.

WHO WAS THOMAS MERTON?

For over fifty years, the thought and writings of Thomas Merton have guided spiritual seekers across the world. His writings offer important insights into four essential relationships—with self, with God, with other people, and with all of creation. While the Christian tradition is the foundation of his perspective, he is open and inclusive in his examination of other religious traditions, recognizing the important contribution that all faith traditions have made throughout the history of civilization. He draws from their strengths to enhance the spiritual growth of individuals and communities.

Thomas Merton was born in Prades, France, in 1915. His mother was from the United States and his father from New Zealand. Educated in France, England, and the United States, he received a master's degree in English from Columbia University. In 1938 he was baptized into the Catholic Church. He taught at St. Bonaventure University for a year and then in 1941 entered the Cistercian Order as a monk of the Abbey of Gethsemani in Kentucky. Directed by his Abbot, Dom Frederic Dunne, Merton wrote his autobiography, *The Seven Storey Mountain*, which was published in 1948.

For fifteen years he served as Master of Scholastics and Novices while writing many books and articles on the spiritual life, inter-religious understanding, peace, and social justice issues. In December of 1968, he journeyed to Asia to attend a conference of contemplatives near Bangkok, Thailand. While there he was accidentally electrocuted and died at the age of fifty-three.

Interest in Merton has grown steadily since his death. *The Seven Storey Mountain* appears on lists of the one hundred most important books of the last century, has been in print ever since its first edition, and has sold millions of copies. The volume of printed work by and about him attests to Merton's popularity. His works have been translated into thirty-five languages and new foreign language editions continue to be printed. The International Thomas Merton Society currently has thirty chapters in the United States and fourteen in other countries.

Thomas Merton is distinguished among contemporary spiritual writers by the depth and substance of his thinking. Merton was a scholar who distilled the best thinking of the best theologians, philosophers, and poets throughout the centuries, from both the West and the East, and presented their ideas in the context of the Christian worldview. His remarkable and enduring popularity indicates that he speaks to the minds and hearts of people searching for answers to life's important questions. For many he is a spiritual guide, and for others he offers a place to retreat to in difficult times. His writings take people into deep places within themselves and offer insight into the paradoxes of life. They wrestle with how to be contemplative in a world of action, yet offer no quick fix or "Ten Easy Steps" to a successful spiritual life.

Using *Bridges* to *Contemplative Living* with *Thomas Merton*

Bridges is intended for anyone seeking to live more contemplatively. For some it initiates a spiritual journey, for others it leads to re-examination or recovery of a neglected spiritual life, and for still others it deepens an already vibrant spirituality. Through reflection and dialogue on specific spiritual themes, participants revisit and refresh their perspectives on and understanding of life. They explore the strength and balance of the relationships that ultimately determine who they are: relationships with self, God, others, and nature. Through examining these relationships, participants probe their understanding of life's great questions:

"Who am I?"

"Who is God?"

"Why am I here?"

"What am I to do with my life?"

The selected readings move participants in and out of four dimensions of contemplative living—*Awakening* to an ever-deepening awareness of "true-self," *Contemplation* of a life experienced from a God-centered perspective, *Compassion* in relationships with others, and *Unity* realized in our undeniable and essential inter-connectedness with all of creation. This fourfold process of spiritual formation frames much of Merton's thought and writing.

This is not a spiritual formation program in some "other-worldly" sense. Merton insists that our spiritual life is our everyday lived experience. There is no separation between them. *Bridges* does not require an academic background in theology, religion, or spirituality, nor does it require use of any particular spiritual practices or prayers. There are no levels of perfection, goals to attain, or measurements of progress. This is not an academic or scholarly undertaking. Everyone will find a particular way of contemplative living within his or her own circumstances, religious tradition, and spiritual practices.

The *Bridges to Contemplative Living with Thomas Merton* series is especially designed for small group dialogue. The selected themes of each session are intended to progressively inform and deepen the relationships that form our everyday lives. Each session begins with scripture and ends in prayer. In between there are time and mental space for spiritual reading, reflection, and contemplative dialogue.

WHAT DO WE MEAN BY CONTEMPLATIVE DIALOGUE?

Contemplative dialogue is meant to be non-threatening, a "safe place" for open sharing and discussion. It is not outcome-oriented. It's not even about fully understanding or comprehending what one reads or hears from the other participants. The focus is on *listening* rather than thinking about how we will respond to what we hear. Simply hearing and accepting another's point of view and reflecting on it can inform and enlighten our own perspective in a way that debating or analyzing it cannot. The pace of conversation is slower in contemplative dialogue than in most other conversations. We are challenged to listen more carefully and approach different points of view by looking at the deeper values and issues underlying them.

EIGHT PRINCIPLES FOR ENTERING INTO CONTEMPLATIVE DIALOGUE

1. Keep in mind that *Bridges* focuses on our "lived experience" and how the session theme connects to everyday life. Keep your comments rooted in your own experience and refrain from remarks that are overly abstract, philosophical, or theoretical.

2. Express your own thoughts knowing they will be heard to be reflected on and not necessarily responded to verbally. It is helpful to use "I" statements like "I believe . . ." or "I am confused by that response." Try framing your remarks with phrases such as "My assumption is that . . ." or "My experience has been . . ."

3. Pay attention to the assumptions, attitudes, and experiences underlying your initial or surface thoughts on the topic. Ask yourself questions like: "Why am I drawn to this particular part of the reading?" "What makes me feel this way?"

4. Remember to listen first and refrain from thinking about how you might respond to another's comments. Simply listen to and accept his or her thoughts on the subject without trying to challenge, critique, or even respond aloud to them.

5. Trust the group. Observe how the participants' ideas, reflections, common concerns, assumptions, and attitudes come together and form a collective group mind.

6. Reflect before speaking and be concise. Make one point or relate one experience then stop and allow others to do the same.

7. Expect periods of silence during the dialogue. Learn to be comfortable with the silence and resist the urge to speak just because there is silence.

8. In time you will adjust to saying something and not receiving a response and to listening without asking a question, challenging, or responding directly. Simply speaking to the theme or idea from your own experience or perspective takes some practice. Be patient with yourself and the other members of your group and watch for deepening levels of dialogue.

ADDITIONAL RESOURCES

A *Leader's Guide* for the *Bridges* series is available from Ave Maria Press.

Online resources available at www.avemariapress.com include:
- Leader's Guide
- Series Sampler
- Suggested Retreat Schedule
- Program Evaluation Form
- Links to other books about Thomas Merton
- Interview with Robert Toth of The Merton Institute for Contemplative Living
- www.mertoninstitute.org

Merton: A Film Biography (1 hour) provides an excellent overview on Merton's life and spiritual journey. The DVD version contains an additional hour of insights from those who knew him.

Contemplation and Action is a periodic newsletter from The Merton Institute with information about new Merton publications, programs, and events. It is free and can be obtained by visiting the Foundation website or calling 1-800-886-7275.

The Thomas Merton Spiritual Development Program is a basic introduction to Merton's life and his insights on contemplative spirituality, social justice, and inter-religious dialogue. Especially designed for youth, it includes a participant's workbook/journal.

WEEKLY MERTON REFLECTIONS

To receive a brief reflection from Merton's works via e-mail each week register at The Merton Institute website www.mertoninstitute.org or by contacting:

The Merton Institute for Contemplative Living
2117 Payne Street
Louisville, KY 40206
1-800-886-7275

session one
CONTEMPLATIVE LIVING

OPENING REFLECTION
PSALM 91:2–3, 5–6

It is good to give thanks to the Lord
to make music to your name, O Most High,
to proclaim your love in the morning
and your truth in the watches of the night.
Your deeds, O Lord, have made me glad,
for the work of your hands I shout for joy.
O Lord, how great are your works!
How deep are your designs.

INTRODUCTION TO THE TEXTS

Gabriel Marcel, the Christian French philosopher, could have been speaking about living contemplatively when he wrote that "Life is not a problem to be solved but a mystery to be lived." Contemplation, as Thomas Merton writes of it, is not a solution to any of our problems, but a way of praying. Contemplative living is a way of being present to our experiences that appreciates the adventure and gift of being alive. Contemplation is not a series of techniques whose aim is to achieve self-calming, although contemplation cannot begin unless one develops a taste for quiet and periods of solitude. Contemplation is experiencing a "still-point" that allows us to recognize the "one thing necessary" for our lives that makes us more deeply joyful and courageous human beings. When we live contemplatively we take a stance on life that enables us to focus and "see" that both simplicity and complexity of experience are equally good and beautiful. Living a life that is contemplative opens us to ourselves, our neighbors, and, at deeper levels that we do not often experience, to God who, Merton would say, has been present to our lives and experience all the time.

MERTON'S VOICE
FROM *NEW SEEDS OF CONTEMPLATION*

Contemplation is life itself, fully awake, fully active, fully aware that it is alive. It is spiritual wonder. It is spontaneous awe at the sacredness of life, of being. It is gratitude for life, for awareness, and for being. It is a vivid realization of the fact that life and being in us proceed from an invisible, transcendent, and infinitely abundant Source. Contemplation is, above all, awareness of the reality of that Source. It *knows* the Source, obscurely, inexplicably, but with a certitude that goes beyond reason and beyond simple faith. . . . It is a more profound depth of faith, a knowledge too deep to be grasped in images, in words, or even in clear concepts. . . .

Contemplation is also the response to a call: a call from Him Who has no voice, and yet Who speaks in everything that is, and Who, most of all, speaks in the depths of our own being: for we ourselves are words of His. But we are words that are meant to respond to Him, to answer to Him, to echo Him, and even in some way to contain Him and signify Him. Contemplation is this echo. It is a deep resonance in the inmost center of our spirit in which our very life loses its separate voice and re-sounds with the majesty and the mercy of the Hidden and Living One. . . .

It is awakening, enlightenment, and the amazing intuitive grasp by which love gains certitude of God's creative and dynamic intervention in our daily life. Hence contemplation does not simply "find" a clear idea of God and confine Him within the limits of that idea, and hold Him there as a prisoner to Whom it can always return. On the contrary, contemplation is carried away by Him into His own realm, His own mystery, and His own freedom (pp. 1–5).

ANOTHER VOICE
PEMA CHODRON, *START WHERE YOU ARE*

We try so hard to hang on to the teachings and "get it," but actually the truth sinks in like rain into very hard earth. The rain is very gentle, and we soften up slowly at our own speed. But when that happens, something has fundamentally changed in us. That hard earth has softened. It doesn't seem to happen by trying to get it or capture it. It happens by letting go; it happens by relaxing your mind, and it happens by the aspiration and the longing to want to communicate with yourself and others. Each of us finds our own way. The very last slogan is "Train wholeheartedly." You could say, "Live wholeheartedly." Let everything stop your mind and let everything open your heart. And you could say, "Die wholeheartedly, moment after moment." Moment after moment let yourself die wholeheartedly (p. 142).

Reflect and Dialogue

Which images, words, or phrases in these readings resonate most with your experience?

How do they make you feel?

What do they mean for your life?

How would you describe for someone else the way you pray?

What would it mean to you if you told yourself that you want to live more contemplatively?

Why are attention and awareness significant for a person who wants to live contemplatively?

Closing

Conclude with one of the prayers on pages 53–55 or with a period of quiet reflection.

session two

CONTEMPLATIVE DIALOGUE

OPENING REFLECTION
FROM PSALM 33

Glorify the Lord with me.
Together let us praise his name.
I sought the Lord and he answered me;
from all my terrors he set me free.
Taste and see that the Lord is good.

INTRODUCTION TO THE TEXTS

The art of dialogue, particularly contemplative dialogue, is less common in our experience than is arguing or discussing. We are not as accustomed to listening as we are to speaking. We often find ourselves thinking what we are going to say while the other person is talking to us. Our natural urge is to be heard, and therefore we are often not fully present to one another when communicating.

Sitting together in silence, pondering these texts together, provides an atmosphere where persons can speak their hearts and minds more freely, out of their personal experience, rather than speaking only what is "expected" to be said or what is "safe" to say. The topics of *Bridges to Contemplative Living* are not ones we often discuss with others; in truth, we may rarely even think about them. Thus, dialoguing contemplatively is not easy and natural to us. It may require us to be patient with ourselves and our partners in dialogue. Gradually, over time and with experience, the words that are truest to who we are will rise up in us and we can speak them out into our shared silence and know that we and our words are being received with attention and respect.

MERTON'S VOICE
FROM *CONJECTURES OF A GUILTY BYSTANDER*

Our thought should not merely be an answer to what somebody else has just said. Or what someone else might have said. Our interior word must be more than an echo of words of someone else. There is no point in being a moon to somebody else's sun, still less is there any justification for our being moons to one another, and hence darkness to one another, not one of us being a true sun. . . .

Would that we could remember how to answer or to keep silence. To learn this, we must learn to go even without answering. One may say: "But to answer is to love." Certainly there is no love without response. But merely to submit one's intelligence, to make a deal, to conciliate, to compromise with error or injustice is not love. Silence, too, is a response. It can at times be the response of a greater love, and of a love that does not endanger truth or sacrifice reasons in order to placate a too demanding or too needy lover.

St. Alphonsus Rodriguez said: "Answer nothing, nothing, nothing" (pp. 99–100).

ANOTHER VOICE
ECKHART TOLLE, *THE POWER OF NOW*

When listening to another person, don't just listen with your mind, listen with your whole body. Feel the energy field of your inner body as you listen. That takes attention away from thinking and creates a still space that enables you to truly listen without the mind interfering. You are giving the other person space—space to be. It is the most precious gift you can give. Most people don't know how to listen because the major part of their attention is taken up by their thinking. They pay more attention to that than to what the other person is saying and none at all to what really matters: the Being of the other person underneath the words and the mind (p. 105).

REFLECT AND DIALOGUE

Which images, words, or phrases in these readings resonate most with your experience?

How do they make you feel?

What do they mean for your life?

Why is it difficult for you to speak deeply with others about personal experiences and about your spiritual perspectives?

What value do we place on silence in our culture and in our everyday lives?

CLOSING

Conclude with one of the prayers on pages 53–55 or with a period of quiet reflection.

session three
EXPLORING LIFE'S QUESTIONS

OPENING REFLECTION
FROM PSALM 118

My soul lies in the dust;
by your word revive me.
I declared my ways and you answered:
teach me your statutes.
Make me grasp the way of your precepts
and I will muse on your wonders.
My soul pines away with grief;
by your word raise me up.
Keep me from the way of error
and teach me your law.
I have chosen the way of truth
with your decrees before me.
I will bind myself to do your will;
Lord, do not disappoint me.
I will run the way of your commands;
you will give freedom to my heart.

INTRODUCTION TO THE TEXTS

In Merton's introduction to *No Man Is An Island*, he observes that we often experience anxiety and insecurity because we are afraid to ask the right questions about life, especially when the right questions might turn out to have no answer: "One of the moral diseases we communicate to one another in society comes from huddling together in the pale light of an insufficient answer to a question we are afraid to ask" (pp. xiii).

In matters of life and death, we often rely on experts or on what we perceive to be the general consensus of opinion within our family and among our closest friends. In matters of war and peace, or during times of insecurity because of rapid social change, we rely on the answers of politicians, think tanks, approved theologians, or the media.

Marshal McLuhan, author of *The Medium Is the Message,* advises us to understand how our senses are being "massaged" to reach the conclusion that those controlling the medium want us to reach. The discipline of entering the silence and raising the right questions that might not have easy answers is an important aspect of the role of contemplation in Merton's life and writing.

MERTON'S VOICE
FROM *THE HIDDEN GROUND OF LOVE*

In 1967 Pope Paul VI asked Thomas Merton to partici-pate in writing a "message from contemplatives" for the people of the world. Merton resisted at first but wrote the following message that was not included in the published statement.

It is true that, when I came to this monastery where I am, I came in revolt against the meaningless confusion of a life in which there was so much activity, so much movement, so much useless talk, so much superficial and needless stimulation, that I could not remember who I was. But the fact remains that my flight from the world is not a reproach to you who remain in the world, and I have no right to repudiate the world in a purely negative fashion, because, if I do that, my flight will have taken me not to truth and to God, but to a private, though doubtless pious, illusion.

Can I tell you that I have found answers to the questions that torment the people of our time? I do not know if I have found answers. When I first became a monk, yes, I was surer of "answers." But as I grow old in the monastic life and advance further into solitude, I become aware that I have only begun to seek the questions. And what are the questions? Can we make sense out of our existence? Can we honestly give our lives meaning merely by adopting a certain set of explanations which pretend to tell us why the world began and where it will end, why there is evil and what is necessary for a good life? My brothers and sisters, perhaps in my solitude I have become, as it were, an explorer for you, a searcher in realms which you are not able to visit—except perhaps in the company of your psychiatrist. I have been summoned to explore a desert area of the human heart in which explanations no longer suffice, and in which one learns that only experience counts. An arid, rocky, dark land of the soul, sometimes illuminated by strange fires which we fear and peopled by specters which we studiously avoid except in our nightmares. And in this area I have learned that one cannot truly know hope unless one has found out how like despair hope is (p. 156).

Another Voice
Ranier Maria Rilke, *Letters to a Young Poet*

I think you will not have to remain without a solution if you trust in things that are like the ones my eyes are now resting upon. If you trust in nature, in what is simple in nature, in the small things that hardly anyone sees and that can so suddenly become huge, immeasurable; if you have this love for what is humble and try very simply, as someone who serves, to win the confidence of what seems poor; then everything will become easier for you, more coherent and somehow more reconciling, not in your conscious mind perhaps, which stays behind, astonished, but in your innermost awareness, awakeness, and knowledge. You are so young, so much before all beginning, and I would like to beg you, dear Sir, as well as I can, to have patience with everything unresolved in your heart and to try to love the questions themselves as if they were locked rooms or books written in a foreign language. Don't search for answers, which could not be given to you now, because you would not be able to live them. And the point is, to live everything. Live the questions now. Perhaps then, someday far in the future, you will gradually, without even noticing it, live your way into the answer. Perhaps you do carry within you the possibility of creating and forming, as an especially blessed and pure way of living; train yourself for that—but take whatever comes, with great trust, and as long as it comes out of your own will, out of some need of your innermost self, then take it upon yourself, and don't hate anything (pp. 33–35).

REFLECT AND DIALOGUE

Which images, words, or phrases in these readings resonate most with your experience?

How do they make you feel?

What do they mean for your life?

Can you articulate one of your life's deepest "hard" questions?

What role do your deepest "hard" questions play in your life?

Do you find yourself and/or others anxious because they cannot accept the "easy" answers we have received from our culture and society?

CLOSING

Conclude with one of the prayers on pages 53–55 or with a period of quiet reflection.

session four
TRUSTING LIFE, NATURE, AND GOD

OPENING REFLECTION
FROM PSALM 115

How can I repay the Lord
for His goodness to me?
The cup of salvation I will raise;
I will call on the Lord's name.

INTRODUCTION TO THE TEXTS

Do we trust life, or are we full of anxiety? Saint Paul
insisted: "Love bears all things, believes all things,
hopes all things, endures all things" (1 Corinthians
13:7). Thomas Merton would agree, but raises this
realistic caution: "In a world where every lie has
currency, is not anxiety the more real and the more
human reaction?" (*No Man Is an Island*, xii–xiii).
Before love takes hold of us and allows us to "hope
all things," we must endure periods of darkness that
may seem like despair, but are in fact periods of
purification. This is when we learn to hope only in
what can consistently give us life. This is when we
learn to trust life.

MERTON'S VOICE
FROM *RAIDS ON THE UNSPEAKABLE*

There is a certain innocence in not having a solution. There is a certain innocence in a kind of

despair, but only if in despair we find salvation. I mean, despair of this world and what is in it. Despair of men and of their plans, in order to hope for the impossible answer that lies beyond our earthly contradictions, and yet can burst into our world and solve them only if there are some who hope in spite of despair.

The true solutions are not those which we force upon life in accordance with our theories, but those which life itself provides for those who dispose themselves to receive the truth. Consequently, our task is to dissociate ourselves from all who have theories which promise clear and infallible solutions, and to mistrust all such theories, not in a spirit of negativism and defeat, but rather trusting life itself, and nature, and if you will permit me, God above all. For since man has decided to occupy the place of God he has shown himself to be by far the blindest, and cruelest, and pettiest, and most ridiculous of all the false gods. We can call ourselves innocent only if we refuse to forget this, and if we also do everything we can to make others realize it (pp. 60–61).

ANOTHER VOICE
ABRAHAM J. HESCHEL, *MAN'S QUEST FOR GOD*

We do not refuse to pray; we abstain from it. We ring the hollow bell of selfishness rather than absorb the stillness that surrounds the world, hovering over all the restlessness and fear of life—the secret stillness that precedes our birth and succeeds our death. Futile self-indulgence brings us out of tune with the gentle song of nature's waiting, of mankind's striving for salvation.

Is not listening to the pulse of wonder worth silence and abstinence from self-asserting? Why do we not set apart an hour of living for devotion to God by surrendering to stillness?

We dwell on the edge of mystery and ignore it, wasting our souls, risking our stake in God. We constantly pour our inner light away from Him, setting up the thick screen of self between Him and us, adding more shadows to the darkness that already hovers between Him and our wayward reason. Accepting surmises as dogmas, and prejudices as solutions, we ridicule the evidence of life for what is more than life. Our mind has ceased to be sensitive to the wonder. . . .

Rushing through the ecstasies of ambition, we only awake when plunged into dread or grief. In darkness, then, we grope for solace, for meaning, for prayer (pp. 4–5).

Reflect and Dialogue

Which images, words, or phrases in these readings resonate most with your experience?

How do they make you feel?

What do they mean for your life?

In times when you experienced darkness, what have you hoped in, what have you placed your trust in?

What does it mean to you to "trust in life and nature"?

Closing

Conclude with one of the prayers on pages 53–55 or with a period of quiet reflection.

session five

PRAYING THROUGH YOUR CHANGING IMAGE OF GOD

OPENING REFLECTION
FROM PSALM 70

In you, O Lord, I take refuge;
let me never be put to shame.
In your justice rescue me, free me:
pay heed to me and save me.
Be a rock where I can take refuge,
a mighty stronghold to save me;
for you are my rock, my stronghold.
Free me from the hand of the wicked,
from the grip of the unjust, of the oppressor.
It is you, O Lord, who are my hope,
my trust, O Lord, since my youth.
On you I have leaned from my birth,
from my mother's womb you have been
my help.
My hope has always been in you.

INTRODUCTION TO THE TEXTS

There comes an important time in your life when
you must own your image of God. Is your God a
philosophical concept that you think about? Is God
a set of moral principles that you adhere to? Is God
a person you relate to and love? Asking yourselves
who God truly is for you and how God "relates"

you to life is a question at the epicenter of a person's spirituality.

Just as our image of ourselves changes with experience and maturation, so our image of God changes over a life's experience. As we mature our self-images become more complex. We become mysteries to ourselves. It is normal and not surprising, but no less frightening, to experience God as more complex and mysterious than we were ever taught.

MERTON'S VOICE
FROM *CONTEMPLATIVE PRAYER*

In meditation we do not seek to know about God as though he were an object like other objects which submit to our scrutiny and can be expressed in clear scientific ideas. We seek to know God himself, beyond the level of all the objects which he has made and which confront us as "things" isolated from one another, "defined," "delimited," with clear boundaries. The infinite God has no boundaries and our minds cannot set limits to him or to his love. His presence is then "grasped" in the general awareness of loving faith; it is "realized" without being scientifically and precisely known, as we know a specimen under a microscope. His presence cannot be verified as we would verify a laboratory experiment. Yet it can be spiritually realized as long as we do not insist on verifying it. As soon as we try to verify the spiritual presence as an object of exact knowledge, God eludes us.

In a word, God is invisibly present to the ground of our being: our belief and love attain to him, but he remains hidden from the arrogant gaze of our investigating mind which seeks to capture him and secure permanent possession of him in an act of knowledge that gives *power over him*. It is in fact absurd and impossible to try to grasp God as an object which can be seized and comprehended by our minds.

The knowledge of which we are capable is simply knowledge *about* him. It points to him in analogies which we must transcend in order to reach him. But we must transcend ourselves as well as our analogies, and in seeking to know him we must forget the familiar subject-object relationship which characterizes our ordinary acts of knowing. Instead, we know him insofar as we become aware of ourselves as known through and through by him. We "possess" him in proportion as we realize ourselves to be possessed by him in the inmost depths of our being. Meditation or "prayer of the heart" is the active effort we make to keep our hearts open so that we may be enlightened by him and filled with this realization of our true relation to him. Therefore the classic form of "meditation" is repetitive invocation of the name of Jesus in the heart emptied of images and cares.

Hence the aim of meditation, in the context of Christian faith, is not to arrive at an objective and apparently "scientific" knowledge about God, but to come to know him through the realization that our very being is penetrated with his knowledge and love for us (pp. 79, 82–83).

ANOTHER VOICE
PIERRE-MARIE DELFIEUX, *THE JERUSALEM COMMUNITY RULE OF LIFE*

Prayer is *difficult*: that you know. It is the very spot where your free giving takes place; the abode of the invisible, often of the unfelt, the incomprehensible, the ineffable, the unexpected. For you, too, it will be hard to love a God whose face you have never seen. . . .

Do not place your happiness in what you can hear or feel of God in prayer but rather in what you can neither feel nor understand. God is always hidden and difficult to find. Go on serving God in this way, as though God were concealed in a sacred place, even when you think you have found God, felt God or heard God. The less you understand, the closer you get to God. Prayer will show you that God is forever the Wholly Other, and you will always fall short.

Prayer will teach you, too, that God is nearer to you than you are to yourself. After passing the fiery crucible and stepping through the narrow doorway where you can bring nothing with you, enter the cave of your heart that contains God, whom the universe cannot hold.

In prayer, then, you will find *peace, light and joy.* There will be the source of your love and the strength of your life. To enlighten your mind, pray. To discern your path, pray. To unify your being, pray. . . . That light may fall on your face and rejoice your heart, pray. To be incorporated into Christ, pray; you no longer live but Christ lives in you. Gradually you will be enlightened, cleansed, purified, matured and joyfully quickened. And so, deified. Filled with your fullness you will be able to enter God's total plenitude. Nothing is left but to contemplate God's glory (pp. 12–13).

Reflect and Dialogue

Which images, words, or phrases in these readings resonate most with your experience?

How do they make you feel?

What do they mean for your life?

How has your image of God changed through your life's experience?

How has your way of praying changed with your altered image of God?

How is your image of God unique to you?

Closing

Conclude with one of the prayers on pages 53–55 or with a period of quiet reflection.

session six
DOING GOD'S WILL

OPENING REFLECTION
FROM PSALM 39

How many, O Lord my God,
are the wonders and designs
that you have worked for us;
you have no equal.
Should I proclaim and speak of them
they are more than I can tell!
You do not ask for sacrifice and offerings,
but an open ear.
You do not ask for holocaust and victim.
Instead, here am I.
In the scroll of the book it stands written
that I should do your will.
My God, I delight in your law
in the depth of my heart.

INTRODUCTION TO THE TEXTS

Merton understood that God's "will" was revealed most personally in the responses demanded of him through his relationships with his neighbors in the widest sense of that reality. Merton's neighbors were all beings with whom he shared his life. Every relationship in which we find ourselves asks us to respond flexibly, with justice and mercy, to what is the often unspoken need of our neighbor.

We live contemplatively so that we can live dynamically in response to the changing needs of the neighbor before us. Contemplative living is a means to discern the "deeper laws of the heart" in relationships that demand our loving kindness beyond what is only legally correct. When we obey these personal requests of our neighbors we respond with justice and mercy, we strive to follow Christ's command to "love one another" in all situations. This is God's will for us.

MERTON'S VOICE
FROM *NEW SEEDS OF CONTEMPLATION*

How am I to know the will of God? Even where there is no other more explicit claim on my obedience, such as a legitimate command, the very nature of each situation usually bears written into itself some indication of God's will. For whatever is demanded by truth, by justice, by mercy, or by love must surely be taken to be willed by God. To consent to His will is, then, to consent to be true, or to speak truth, or at least to seek it. To obey Him is to respond to His will expressed in the need of another person, or at least to respect the rights of others. For the right of another man is the expression of God's love and God's will. In demanding that I respect the rights of another, God is not merely asking me to conform to some abstract, arbitrary law: He is enabling me to share, as His Son, in His own care for my brother. No man who ignores the rights and needs of others can hope to walk in the light of contemplation, because his way has turned aside from truth, from compassion and therefore from God.

The requirements of a work to be done can be understood as the will of God. If I am supposed to hoe a garden or make a table, then I will be obeying God if I am true to the task I am performing. To do the work carefully and well, with love and respect for the nature of my task and with due attention to its purpose, is to unite myself to God's will in my work. In this way I become His instrument. He works through me. When I act as His instrument my labor cannot become an obstacle to contemplation, even though it may temporarily so occupy my mind that I cannot engage in it while I am actually doing my job. Yet my work itself will purify and pacify my mind and dispose me for contemplation (pp. 18–19).

If you want to know what is meant by "God's will" in man's life, this is one way to get a good idea of it. "God's will" is certainly found in anything that is required of us in order that we may be united with one another in love. You can call this, if you like, the basic tenet of the Natural Law, which is that we should treat others as we would like them to treat us, that we should not do to another what we would not want another to do to us (p. 76).

ANOTHER VOICE
WILKIE AU, *BY WAY OF THE HEART*

Unfortunately, many people view the will of God as rather like a ten-ton elephant hanging overhead, ready to fall on them. . . . Actually the word which we translate into English as *will* comes from both a Hebrew and a Greek word which means *yearning*. It

38

is that yearning which lovers have for one another. Not a yearning of the mind alone or of the heart alone but of the whole being. A yearning which we feel is only a glimmering of the depth of the yearning of God for us.

Thus, the will of God is dynamic, personal love urging us along the path that leads to union with the Lord. As with an ordinary journey, there may be several paths that can lead equally well to our destination; or some way may be notably better; or some way may lead us away from our destination. So, "the prayer to know God's will," states theologian John Wright, "is a prayer to have this kind of insight about the choices open to me." When we pray "Your will be done," we are not thinking about a script of our lives God has destined from all eternity. Rather we are referring to the choices we must make. And when these lead to union with God, they are compatible with God's plan to unite all creation. "Thus, it may sometime happen that I will actually be doing God's will, following the guidance of the Holy Spirit, whether I choose this or that" (pp. 67–68).

REFLECT AND DIALOGUE

Which images, words, or phrases in these readings resonate most with your experience?

How do they make you feel?

What do they mean for your life?

Do you have a personal way of discerning God's will for yourself?

What if God's will only required for us to make creative choices in every situation?

What is the most immediate way for you to discover God's will in your life?

CLOSING

Conclude with one of the prayers on pages 53–55 or with a period of quiet reflection.

session seven

Praying Out of the Roots of Your Own Life

Opening Reflection
From Psalm 138

> For it was you who created my being,
> knit me together in my mother's womb.
> I thank you for the wonder of my being,
> for the wonders of all your creation.
> Already you knew my soul,
> my body held no secret from you
> when I was being fashioned in secret
> and molded in the depths of the earth.
> Your eyes saw all my actions,
> they were all of them written in your book;
> every one of my days was decreed
> before one of them came into being.

Introduction to the Texts

Someone taught us to pray. Someone taught us the concepts of "success" and "failure" in living our lives. But moments come when everything one has been taught has to be more personally owned or disowned. Moments come that force us to question our lives more deeply and instigate a change of heart and mind. At these moments we begin to pray, as Merton wrote in his autobiography that he prayed in Rome at sixteen, "not with my lips and with my intellect and my imagination, but praying out of the very roots of my life and of my being, and praying to the God I had never known."

Moments of *metanoia*, when our souls change, are moments of sadness or happiness that turn us to living more deeply, consciously embracing our vocations as persons of faith. We are not "struck off our horses" once and for all as St. Paul was, but experience these moments of continuing conversion all the time, every day. Contemplative living is an attitude of open responsiveness to hearing these "new words" that God wants us to hear through our life-stories. We remain open and pray to be changed into the person God calls us to be.

MERTON'S VOICE
FROM *DANCING IN THE WATER OF LIFE*

The great joy of the solitary life is not found simply in quiet, in the beauty and peace of nature, song of birds, etc. nor in the peace of one's own heart, but in the awakening and attuning of the heart to the voice of God—to the inexplicable, quiet, definite inner certitude of one's call to obey Him, to hear Him, to worship Him here, now, today, in silence and alone, and that this is the whole reason for one's existence, this makes one's existence fruitful and gives fruitfulness to all one's other (good) acts, and is the ransom and purification of one's heart that has been dead in sin.

It is not simply a question of "existing" alone, but of doing, with joy and understanding, "the work of the cell" [the work of contemplative solitude] which is done in silence and not according to one's own choice or the pressure of necessity but in obedience to God. But the voice of God is not "heard" at every moment, so part of the "work of the cell" is attention so that one may not miss any sound of that Voice. When we see how little we listen, and how stubborn and gross our hearts are, we realize how important the work is and how badly prepared we are to do it (pp. 254–255).

ANOTHER VOICE
PAUL EVDOKIMOV, *THE AGES OF THE SPIRITUAL LIFE*

With rare exceptions, the spiritual life comes into being in an event that is called "conversion." Its precise content is of little importance. It is a remarkable event, a shock followed by a sharply defined passage from one state to another. Just as light reveals shadows, it suddenly unveils the inadequacy of the unstable present and leads us to doors opening upon a new world. This beginning of an untried promise leads to decisive actions and entails the joyful commitment of our whole being. Even those who inherited the faith in their childhood pass sooner or later through this by a conscious discovery of their faith, and by appropriating it to themselves personally. This is always an overwhelming experience.

Something we have read, an encounter, a reflection, causes a light to break forth suddenly, brilliantly. In its brightness, all is seen in its true order as in an inspired poem that gives to everything a new and inestimable value, as in the music of Mozart. It is a religious springtime, full of joy and enthusiasm. Like the buds filled with sap, the human being feels uplifted in a surprising joy and a spontaneous sympathy for everything and everyone. This is an unforgettable time. Like a feast illumined by a thousand lights, it makes one see God, the smiling countenance of the Father, coming to meet his child (p. 75).

Reflect and Dialogue

Which images, words, or phrases in these readings resonate most with your experience?

How do they make you feel?

What do they mean for your life?

Reflect on a moment in your recent past or present that has invited you to turn more directly toward God.

Can you sense an upcoming situation that could well require another conversion, another changing of your mind and heart?

Closing

Conclude with one of the prayers on pages 53–55 or with a period of quiet reflection.

session eight
COMPASSION: PRAYER IN ACTION

OPENING REFLECTION
FROM PSALM 44

The Lord is kind and full of compassion,
slow to anger, abounding in love.
How good is the Lord to all,
compassionate to all his creatures.
The Lord is faithful in all his words
and loving in all his deeds.
The Lord supports all who fall
and raises all who are bowed down.
The Lord is just in all his ways
and loving in all his deeds.
He is close to all who call him,
who call to him from their hearts.

INTRODUCTION TO THE TEXTS

The hallmark of contemplative living is a deepening ability to respond compassionately to all beings in all situations of our lives. Contemplative living is not narcissism; it is not navel-gazing at the expense of ignoring the suffering of our neighbors. Contemplative living incites an inner struggle against whatever forces within us act as obstacles to our being present to the needs of our neighbors. Through contemplative living we work with and clarify any distortions in our minds and hearts that allow us to misperceive and disregard, to overlook and ignore, and to make invisible our neighbor's need for our recognition and our fellowship. Contemplative living gives our neighbors their just, true, and merciful place in our prayers and within our life's plans.

MERTON'S VOICE
FROM *CONJECTURES OF A GUILTY BYSTANDER*

Night watch. Even though I am Novice Master and am in the novitiate all the time, the novitiate takes on a great air of mystery and revelation when I pass through it on the night watch. . . .

As I was going through absent-mindedly on my round, I pushed open the door of the novices' scriptorium and flashed the light over the desks, and the empty room spoke again. I stood there for a long time before going up to the chapel. Four long rows of desks. Their desks are all they have that is more or less "theirs." It is there that they sit reading, writing, thinking whatever is most personal, most truly their own. They keep their letters, their own few books, their own notes there.

Looking at the dark empty room, with everyone gone, it seemed that, because all that they loved was there, "they" in a spiritual way were most truly there, though in fact they were all upstairs in the dormitory, asleep.

It was as if their love and their goodness had transformed the room and filled it with a presence curiously real, comforting, perfect: one might say, with Christ. Indeed, it seemed to me momentarily that He was as truly present here, in a certain way, as upstairs in the Chapel. The loveliness of the humanity which God has taken to Himself in love is, after all, to be seen in the humanity of our friends, our children, our brothers, the people we love and who love us. Now that God has become Incarnate, why do we go to such lengths, all the time, to "disincarnate" Him again, to unweave the garment of flesh and reduce Him once again to spirit? As if the Body of the Lord had not become "Life-giving Spirit."

You can see the beauty of Christ in each individual person, in that which is most his, most human, most personal to him, in things which an ascetic might advise you sternly to get rid of. But these attachments, too, are relevant to your life in Christ. . . . In any case, I felt there was something quite final and eternal in looking at this empty room: that though they themselves might not understand what they are going through, and though many of them may fail, may leave, or may have to look elsewhere to get the real meaning of their lives, yet the sign of love is on these novices and they are precious forever in God's eyes.

From this basic experience one can, after all, recover hope for the other dimension of man's life: the political. Even though we have the power to destroy the whole world, life is stronger than the death instinct and love is stronger than hate. It does not make logical sense to be too hopeful, but once again this is not a question of logic and one does not look for signs of hope in the newspapers or the pronouncements of world leaders (in these there is seldom anything really hopeful, and that which is supposed to be encouraging is usually so transparently hopeless that it moves one closer to despair). Because there is love in the world, and because Christ has taken our nature to Himself, there remains always hope that man will finally, after many mistakes and even disasters, learn to disarm and make peace, recognizing that he *must* live at peace with his brother. Yet never have we been less disposed to do this.

The fact remains that this is the one great lesson we have to learn. Everything else is trivial compared with this supreme and urgent need of man (pp. 212–214).

ANOTHER VOICE

KAREN ARMSTRONG, *THE SPIRAL STAIRCASE*

In the course of my studies, I have discovered that the religious quest is not about discovering "the truth" or "the meaning of life," but about living as intensely as possible here and now. The idea is not to latch on to some superhuman personality or to "get to heaven" but to discover how to be fully human . . . (pp. 270–271).

For me religion was still essentially about belief. Because I did not accept the orthodox doctrines, I considered myself an agnostic—even an atheist. But by unwittingly putting into practice two of the essential principles of religion, I had already, without realizing it, embarked on a spiritual quest. First, I had set off by myself on my own path. Second, I had at last been able to acknowledge my own pain and feel it fully. I was gradually, imperceptibly being transformed.

All the world's faiths put suffering on the top of their agenda, because it is an inescapable fact of human life, and unless you see things as they really are, you cannot live correctly. But even more important, if we deny our own pain, it is all too easy to dismiss the suffering of others. Every single one of the major traditions—Confucianism, Buddhism and Hinduism, as well as the monotheisms—teaches a spirituality of empathy, by means of which you relate your own suffering to that of others. This, I was to discover, was the essence of religious life (pp. 271–272).

. . . the religious traditions are in unanimous agreement that the one and only test of a valid religious idea, doctrinal statement, spiritual experience, or devotional practice was that it must lead directly to practical compassion. If your understanding of the divine makes you kinder, more empathetic, and impels you to express this sympathy in concrete acts of loving-kindness, this was good theology. But if your notion of God made you unkind, belligerent, cruel, or self-righteous, or if it led you to kill in God's name, it was bad theology. Compassion was the litmus test for the prophets of Israel, for the rabbis of the Talmud, for Jesus, for Paul, and for Muhammad, not to mention Confucius, Lao-Tzu, the Buddha, or the sages of the Upanishads . . . (p. 293).

REFLECT AND DIALOGUE

Which images, words, or phrases in these readings resonate most with your experience?

How do they make you feel?

What do they mean for your life?

What barriers have made it difficult for you to be compassionate to those beyond the intimate circle of your personal experience?

What are the forces that cause you not to see other persons as your neighbors?

How can living contemplatively contribute to our living "as if" everyone were your neighbor?

CLOSING

Conclude with one of the prayers on pages 53–55 or with a period of quiet reflection.

CONCLUDING PRAYERS

A

My Lord God,
I have no idea where I am going. I do not see the
road ahead of me. I cannot know for certain where
it will end. Nor do I really know myself, and the fact
that I think I am following your will does not mean
that I am actually doing so. But I believe that the
desire to please You does in fact please You. And I
hope I have that desire in all that I am doing. I hope
that I will never do anything apart from that desire.
And I know that, if I do this, You will lead me by the
right road, though I may know nothing about it.
Therefore I will trust You always though I may seem
to be lost and in the shadow of death. I will not fear,
for You are ever with me, and You will never leave
me to face my perils alone.

Thomas Merton
Thoughts in Solitude, p. 83

B

Grant us Prudence in proportion to our power.
Wisdom in proportion to our science and
Humaneness in proportion to our wealth and
might. Bless our earnest will to help all races and
people to travel in friendship along the road to justice, liberty and lasting peace.

Grant us above all to see that our ways are not necessarily Your ways, that we cannot fully penetrate the mystery of Your designs and that the very storm of power now raging on this earth reveals Your hidden will and Your inscrutable decision. Grant us to see Your face in the lightning of this cosmic storm, O God of holiness, merciful to all. Grant us to seek peace where it is truly found!

In Your will, O God, is our peace!

Amen.

Thomas Merton
The Nonviolent Alternative, pp. 269–270

C

O God we are one with You.

You have made us one with You. You have taught us that if we are open to one another, You dwell in us. Help us to realize that there can be no understanding where there is mutual rejection. O God, in accepting one another wholeheartedly, fully, completely, we accept You, and we thank You, and we adore You, and we love You with our whole being, because our being is in Your being, our spirit is rooted in Your spirit. Fill us then with love, and let us be bound together with love as we go our diverse ways, united in this one spirit which makes You present in the world, and which You witness to the ultimate reality that is love. Love has overcome. Love is victorious.

Amen.

Thomas Merton
The Asian Journal of Thomas Merton, pp. 318–319

D

When my tongue is silent, I can rest in the silence of the forest. When my imagination is silent, the forest speaks to me, tells me of its unreality and of the Reality of God. But when my mind is silent, then the forest suddenly becomes magnificently real and blazes transparently with the Reality of God. For now I know that the Creation, which first seems to reveal Him in concepts, then seems to hide Him by the same concepts, finally *is revealed in Him*, in the Holy Spirit. And we who are in God find ourselves united in Him with all that springs from Him. This is prayer, and this is glory!

Thomas Merton
Entering the Silence: Becoming a Monk and Writer,
p. 471

SOURCES

The readings from the Psalms are from *The Psalms*. Arranged by Joseph Gelineau. New York/Mahwah: Paulist Press, 1966.

FROM THOMAS MERTON

The Asian Journal of Thomas Merton. New York: New Directions, 1973.

Conjectures of a Guilty Bystander. Garden City, NY: Doubleday, 1966.

Contemplative Prayer. Garden City, NY: Doubleday Image Book, 1969.

Dancing in the Water of Life: Seeking Peace in the Hermitage (The Journals of Thomas Merton, Vol. 5). Robert E. Daggy, ed. San Francisco: HarperSanFrancisco, 1998.

Entering the Silence: Becoming a Monk and Writer. Jonathan Montaldo, ed. San Francisco: HarperSanFrancisco, 1996.

The Hidden Ground of Love. Selected and edited by William H. Shannon. New York: Farrar, Straus & Giroux, 1985.

New Seeds of Contemplation. New York: New Directions, 1962.

The Nonviolent Alternative. New York: Farrar, Straus, Giroux, 1980.

Raids on the Unspeakable. New York: New Directions, 1966.

Thoughts in Solitude. New York: Farrar, Straus & Cudahy, 1958.

OTHER VOICES

Armstrong, Karen. *The Spiral Staircase: My Climb Out of Darkness.* New York: Anchor Books, 2004.

Au, Wilkie. *By Way of the Heart.* Mahwah, NJ: Paulist Press, 1989.

Chodron, Pema. *Start Where You Are: A Guide to Compassionate Living.* Boston: Shambhala Publications, 2001.

Delfieux, Pierre-Marie. *The Jerusalem Community Rule of Life.* Translated from the French by Kathleen England. New York: Paulist Press, 1985.

Evdokimov, Paul. *The Ages of the Spiritual Life.* Revised Translation by Michael Plekon and Alexis Vinogradov. Crestwood, NY: St. Vladimir's Seminary Press, 1998.

Heschel, Abraham J. *Man's Quest for God.* New York: MacMillan Publishing Company, 1974.

Rilke, Rainer Maria. *Letters to a Young Poet.* Translated by Stephen Mitchell. New York: Vintage Books, 1986.

Tolle, Eckhart. *The Power of Now: A Guide to Spiritual Enlightenment.* Novato, CA: New World Library, 2004.

another voice
BIOGRAPHICAL SKETCHES

VOLUME I

Karen Armstrong is the author of several best-selling books, including: *A History of God; Muhammad;* and *Islam, a Short History*. She has been honored as a bridge builder who promotes understanding among the three Abrahamic faiths—Judaism, Christianity, and Islam.

Wilkie Au is the author of the popular titles *By Way of the Heart* and *Urgings of the Heart*. He is a spiritual director in Los Angeles in private practice and teaches in the Department of Theological Studies at Loyola-Marymount University.

Pema Chodron is an ordained *bhikshuni*, or Buddhist nun, in the Tibetan tradition. She lives at Gampo Abbey, a monastic center in the Cape Breton Highlands of Nova Scotia. She is the author of *Wisdom of No Escape, Start Where You Are*, and *When Things Fall Apart*.

Fr. Pierre-Marie Delfieux, a former chaplain at the Sorbonne (University of Paris), founded the Monastic Jerusalem Communities which strive to harmonize a monastic life of prayer and asceticism with office work and business, even in big cities. Its rule *The Jerusalem Rule of Life*, is based on Holy Scripture.

Paul Evdokimov was among the founding members of the Russian Christian Students' Movement in France. During the Nazi occupation there he worked with the resistance and then directed hostels for the care of the poor, refugees, and distressed. A theologian with experience in pastoral and service work, he was an observer at Vatican II and became an important voice for the Eastern Church in the West.

Abraham Heschel was Professor of Jewish Ethics and Mysticism from 1946-72 at the Jewish Theological Seminary of America. He was a civil rights activist and one of the few Jewish writers to be widely read by members of all denominations of Judaism and Christianity. His works include *Man Is Not Alone, God in Search of Man, The Sabbath,* and *The Prophets.*

Rainer Maria Rilke (d. 1926) is considered one of the greatest lyric poets of modern Germany. His works include, *Letters to a Young Poet, Duino Elegies, Sonnets to Orpheus, Rilke's Book of Hours: Love Poems to God,* and *Rilke on Love and Other Difficulties.*

Eckhart Tolle was born in Germany and educated at the Universities of London and Cambridge. At the core of his writings is the transformation of individual and collective human consciousness—a global spiritual awakening. He is author of *The Power of Now.*

about

THE EDITORS

The Merton Institute for Contemplative Living is dedicated to personal spiritual transformation through raising awareness of Merton's spiritual insights and contemplative practices. Their purpose is to promote his vision for a just and peaceful world.

Robert G. Toth has served as the executive director of the Merton Institute since 1998. He is the editor of the *Contemplation and Action* newsletter and wrote the foreword to *Thomas Merton: An Introduction* by William H. Shannon.

Jonathan Montaldo is the associate director of The Merton Institute for Contemplative Living. He is the former director of the Thomas Merton Center at Bellarmine University and past president of the International Thomas Merton Society. Montaldo edited *Entering the Silence,* the *Merton Journals, Volume 2* (1996) and *The Intimate Merton: His Life from His Journals* (1999) with Br. Patrick Hart. He published *Dialogues with Silence: Thomas Merton's Prayers & Drawings* (2001); *Merton & Hesychasm: The Prayer of the Heart* (2003) and *A Year with Thomas Merton: Daily Reflections from His Journals* (2005).

bridges to contemplative living
with thomas merton

Bridges to Contemplative Living with Thomas Merton gently leads participants on a journey toward spiritual transformation and a more contemplative and peace-filled life. Each eight-session booklet provides an introduction to Merton and contemplative living through prayers, readings from Merton and other spiritual masters, and questions for small group dialogue.

A free series Leader's Guide is available for download at www.avemariapress.com or at 1.800.282.1865

Booklets in the Series

bridges to
contemplative living
with thomas merton

edited by
jonathan montaldo & robert g. toth
of the merton institute for contemplative living

One: Entering the School of Your Experience
ISBN: 9781594710896 / 64 pages / $5.95

Two: Becoming Who You Already Are
ISBN: 9781594710902 / 64 pages / $5.95

Three: Living Your Deepest Desires
ISBN: 9781594710926 / 64 pages / $5.95

Four: Discovering the Hidden Ground of Love
ISBN: 9781594710926 / 64 pages / $5.95

Five: Traveling Your Road to Joy
ISBN: 9781594710933 / 64 pages / $5.95

Six: Writing Yourself into the Book of Life
ISBN: 9781594710940 / 64 pages / $5.95

Seven: Adjusting Your Life's Vision
(Available Spring 2008)
ISBN: 9781594710957 / 64 pages / $5.95

Eight: Seeing That Paradise Begins Now
(Available Spring 2008)
ISBN: 9781594710964 / 5.95

ave maria press®

Available from your bookstore or from
ave maria press / Notre Dame, IN 46556
www.avemariapress.com / Ph: 800-282-1865
A Ministry of the Indiana Province of Holy Cross

Keycode: FØAØ8Ø7ØØØØ